The Christmas Book

THE
CHRISTMAS BOOK

Written and illustrated by
ESME EVE

CHATTO & WINDUS

Published by

Chatto & Windus Ltd
40–42 William IV Street. London W.C.2

★

Clarke, Irwin & Co Ltd
Toronto

534314
⅃394·26

ISBN 0 7011 0341 8

Printed and bound in Great Britain by
Redwood Burn Limited, Trowbridge & Esher

Contents

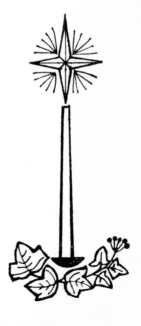

He neither shall be born
  In houses nor in hall,
Nor in the place of paradise
  But in an ox's stall.

He neither shall be christened
  In white wine nor in red,
But with fair spring water
  As we were christenéd.

           A very old carol

J oseph went up to Judaea . . . and with him went Mary who was betrothed to him. She was expecting a child, and while they were there the time came for her baby to be born, and she gave birth to a son, her first-born. She wrapped him in his swaddling clothes, and laid him in a manger, because there was no room for them to lodge in the house.

Now in this same district there were shepherds out in the fields, keeping watch through the night over their flock, when suddenly there stood before them an angel of the Lord, and the splendour of the Lord shone round them. They were terror-stricken, but the angel said, 'Do not be afraid; I have good news for you: there is great joy coming to the whole people. Today in the city of David a deliverer has been born to you—the Messiah, the Lord. And this is your sign: you will find a baby lying wrapped in his swaddling clothes, in a manger.' All at once there was with the angel a great company of heavenly host, singing the praises of God:

'Glory to God in highest heaven,
And on earth his peace for men on whom his favour
    rests.'

After the angels had left them and gone into heaven the shepherds said to one another, 'Come, we must go straight to Bethlehem and see this thing that has happened, which the Lord has made known to us.' So they went with all speed and found their way to Mary and Joseph; and the baby was lying in the manger.

The Gospel according to Saint Luke, Chapter 2, verses 4 to 16
New English Bible, New Testament, Second edition © 1970
by permission of Oxford and Cambridge University Presses

I

Christmas round the World

At the time of the winter solstice, about December 22nd, when the sun appeared to stand still in the sky, when the days were short and the weather bleak, ceremonies used to be held in honour of the Sun-Boar.

Until the return of the sun and the life-renewing warmth of spring, fire, which radiated heat and light, became a substitute and was worshipped by primitive peoples.

The coldness of winter destroyed the pasturage, and herds had to be killed off; but the carcasses were roasted and great feasts were held, and for a short while cold, darkness and hunger were forgotten in the Yuletide celebrations. The Scandinavian word Yule possibly comes from *Jiuleis* or *Giuli*, the name given to the feasts held around November 12th in the Teutonic and Celtic calendars and gradually adopted by the rest of Europe.

At Stonehenge in Britain, the Celtic Druids held their ceremonies and blessed their sacred plant, the mistletoe, from which they prepared a drink as a remedy for poisons. In modern times, mistletoe has very different associations.

The Romans too had feasts and merrymaking in honour of their god Saturn between December 17th and 28th. It was a time of fairs, banquets, dancing and gift-giving. Hymns were sung in praise of the god, and slaves enjoyed a brief period of freedom.

December 25th was universally accepted as Christmas Day in the fourth century and was observed in Rome in A.D. 336.

The Magi or Wise Men who brought gifts to the Christ Child on the first Christmas have continued to figure in custom and legend in all Christian countries down the centuries: the white-bearded, aged Melchior with his gift of gold, the young, dark-skinned Kaspar with his offering of frankincense, and the black-bearded Balthazar with his present of myrrh.

Father Christmas or Santa Claus probably has his origins in pagan times when the supreme god in Scandinavian mythology, Odin or Woden, was worshipped and revered for his great wisdom and military prowess. Legend also has it that he was king of Sweden. He was depicted as an aged bearded man of noble bearing with one all-seeing eye, riding through the dark arctic winters on his white, eight-footed steed Sleipner. Odin's venerable aspect and his white horse recur in many representations of Father Christmas and Saint Nicholas.

Saint Nicholas (Sante Klaas, Nicklaus or Kris Kringle) is identified with the Bishop of Myra, an important town in Lycia, Asia Minor, in the time of the Roman Emperor Diocletian of the third century. Saint Nicholas was persecuted for his Christian faith and is the special protector of children and young people, and he is remembered for his gifts to the poor. Legend says that he saved three destitute sisters from being sold into slavery and gave each of them a bag of gold so that they could be independent. He also restored to life three boys murdered by an innkeeper who hid their bodies in a tub of brine. Thus was started the giving of presents to children on the Eve of Saint Nicholas's Day, December 6th. When the Dutch colonists settled in the United States of America they took this custom with them, and their *Sinterklaas* became Santa Klaus; the giving of presents was later transferred to Christmas Eve, but many European countries still make their distribution of gifts on the Eve of Saint Nicholas's Day. Saint Nicholas

8

arrives in Holland by water. He is a venerable white-bearded figure in a bishop's scarlet cope and mitre, and it is accepted that he has journeyed from Spain. This legend can be traced back to the sixteenth century when the Spanish dominated the Low Countries, and is borne out by the Elizabethan doublet and hose worn by his attendants and in particular by his Moorish servant, Black Peter, who carries a sack in which he is said to put children who have misbehaved during the past twelve months for deportation to Spain. The saint disembarks at Amsterdam and mounts a white horse for a processional ride through the streets of the city. He hears children recite their catechism and may deliver a short homily before distributing gifts.

At one time the spirit of winter and the spirit of Christmas were synonymous, and were depicted by a small gnome-like figure in red tights, almost spherical with

white hair and a long white beard. He wore a wreath of holly. Very similar is the tiny man called Jultomten who brings gifts in Sweden, or the little people named Julnissar who sometimes undertake this work for him. It was American illustrators who gradually evolved the image of Santa Claus or Father Christmas that we accept today, increasing his stature and replacing the holly wreath by a fur-edged cap.

Father Christmas was already a recognised figure in mummers' plays in fifteenth-century England, not only as a personification of Christmas, but also as a bringer of gifts:

In comes I, Father Christmas,
Welcome or welcome not,
I hope old Father Christmas
Will never be forgot.

A carol of this time begins:

Hail, Father Christmas,
Hail to thee.

And another sung about 1520 speaks of Sir Christèmas.

During Puritan days, he was described by one writer as a very old 'grey-bearded gentleman called Christmas, who was wont to be a familiar guest and to visit all sorts of people, both poor and rich'. Cromwell's Commonwealth banned him, along with all other forms of festivity.

In his poem for children, *The Night before Christmas*, written in 1822, Dr Clement Clarke Moore gave names to all Santa's reindeer, and they have been known by these names ever since.

In Sweden Santa Claus is believed to be drawn in his sleigh by mountain goats instead of the usual reindeer.

According to the Swiss, Santa's wife is Lucy or Mother Christmas—a link with Saint Lucia. Another connection with Saint Lucia is the legend in Bohemia that a nanny goat named Lucy brings presents to the children.

On Christmas Eve people in Spain go to 'The Mass of the Cock' at midnight, after which they join in procession through the streets, carrying torches, drums, tambourines and guitars, dancing and singing until the early hours of the morning. One of their favourite carols is the Catalan *Fum, fum, fum*, which stresses the rhythm of the guitars. A similar procession takes place at Epiphany, when the people go out with torches and bells to seek and guide the Wise Men from the East. Straw is strewn upon the ground to prepare the way for the kings' horses, and children leave their shoes on the window-sills or balconies to be filled with gifts. Another Spanish carol sung during torch-light processions is *Torches, torches, run with torches all the way to Bethlehem*.

In the cathedral of Palma on the Mediterranean island of Majorca, a boy dressed as a priest sings the story of the Nativity from the pulpit during the Midnight Mass.

A female counterpart of Santa Claus, called Befana (or Epiphania), is commemorated in Italy. She fills the stockings of good children with gifts on the Eve of the Epiphany or Twelfth Night, but naughty children are threatened that Befana will eat them. Legend tells how Befana was too busy attending to her household duties to find time to entertain the Three Wise Men on their way to Bethlehem. She said she would see them on their return journey, but the Magi went back another way and Befana was punished by being made to seek the Christ Child eternally. In her search she leaves a present at every house where a child lives.

In Florence it was an old custom to herald the arrival of Befana with trumpets, processions and bonfires. In Rome people still congregate in the main square amid great rejoicing and fun.

The Yule log in Italy is lit by blindfolded children, who then beat it with tongs. A juniper fire is lit under the log and money is placed on top of it as a gift to the servants. The ashes are used as a protection against hail and to protect silkworms, silk-weaving being one of the industries of the country.

In the Alps of northern Italy, Bishop Nicholas's way is cleared of snow by two men dressed in straw, who lash the path clear with long whips. They are the ghosts of the field. After them comes a man with a goat's head, followed by a masked and horned demon carrying a birch to chastise sinners, particularly bad women.

A character called Knight Rupprecht comes to hear the children's prayers in north Germany and to distribute gifts. He looks a fierce, rough man, dressed in straw or skins, and for this reason is sometimes called *Ru-Klas* (rough Nicholas). Sometimes he is accompanied by Saint Nicholas. In some districts Saint Peter or the Archangel Gabriel comes with Saint Nicholas.

January 6th, Epiphany, is celebrated as the day the Magi came to Bethlehem (Epiphany meaning 'showing'—that is, the showing of the Christ Child to the Wise Men). For the week following Epiphany, groups of boys, led by one carrying a gold star on a pole, and three others representing the Three Kings—one with a blackened face—proceed through the village, singing carols known as Star-songs.

In Germany a piece of the Yule log is kept to ignite the log of the following Christmas, and the ashes are saved to spray over crops, to protect them from disease. A Greek custom is to burn a Yule log to scare away the spirit-souls of the dead, which are thought to take the visible form of imps called Kallikantzaroi.

On Christmas Eve in Westphalia a table near the Christmas tree is set with soup plates, one for each child of the house. These are filled with sweets overnight by the silently passing Christ Child (*das Christkinde*). Children write Him letters and leave them on the window-sill so that He may read them and grant their wishes.

In Bavaria Saint Nicholas is attended by the *Nikolo-Weibl*, who is a boy dressed as a girl, and by twelve young men dressed in straw, who wear animal masks or skins over their head and cowbells tied about their person. These are the *Buttenmandln*, bearers of good luck; but they handle the occupants of the houses roughly and create a great deal of uproar. The *Nikolo-Weibl* distributes the gifts. Another custom in Bavaria is to place a small Christmas tree on each new grave.

Austrian farm-houses and farm-buildings are blessed with holy water and incense on Christmas Eve. The farmer then visits his barns and stables to sprinkle holy water on each animal, saying, 'Saint Thomas preserve thee from all sickness.' December 21st is the feast-day of Saint Thomas. On this day he is believed to drive in a fiery chariot to churchyards, calling all men named Thomas from their graves to kneel with him round the churchyard cross, which glows red. He blesses his namesakes and then vanishes; and they return to their rest.

Another Austrian tradition was for people to go round the orchards, knocking on fruit trees, commanding them to bear a good harvest in the coming year. At Christmas time and particularly on January 6th it is usual in the Tirol for the head of the family to walk from room to room carrying an open pan of glowing charcoal and incense, fumigating all evil from the house. As each room is purified, so he chalks on the door the initials K+M+B (for the names of Kaspar, Melchior and Balthazar with crosses between them).

13

In Germany and Alsace a girl called Christkindl or Christkinde distributes gifts on behalf of the Holy Child. She has golden wings, is dressed in white and, to create an air of mystery, is usually veiled, although sometimes she wears a crown of lighted candles. She is presumed to enter the house by the window and the cold air of a winter's night accompanies her arrival.

The Christkindl rings a silver bell and carries a basket of gifts. With her comes Han Trapp, an unkempt demon with blackened face and dressed in the skin of a bear who threatens naughty children with a big stick.

The children of France leave *sabots* (wooden shoes) on the hearth to receive presents from *Père Noël* on Christmas Eve. The Christmas Yule log is cut from a plum or cherry tree and is carried into the house by the whole family, starting with the eldest and ending with the youngest. They walk round the kitchen three times and lay the log on the hearth. The father or head of the family pours wine over it, saying, 'Joy, joy, may God shower joy upon us, my dear children. Christmas brings us all good things. God give us grace to see the New Year, and if we do not increase in numbers, may we at all events not decrease.' The part of the log not burnt is shaped into a wedge for the plough, as this is believed to make seed fertile and to cause poultry to thrive.

In Provence one finds the usual Christmas crib in the church or in the house. An old shepherd and a young shepherd boy carry a lamb to church and lay it in the straw beside the crib, which is surrounded with lighted candles, as in the Provençal carol featuring light:

Torches here, Jeanette, Isabella,
Torches here to His cradle bring.

Despite the occasional suppression of the Midnight Mass

of Christmas Eve, because of its pagan origins, this ceremony has been handed down intact at Les Baux in Provence from medieval days, when the Princes of Baux, who claimed descent from one of the three Magi, Balthazar, ruled that district of wild, fantastic rock formation.

The congregation enters the Church of Saint Vincent in procession, led by three men playing pipes and tabors, and by shepherdesses in traditional costume of dark silk gown, long cloak, white lace cap with a wide ribbon and brocade band. Then they sing this carol:

> *As I went on my way,*
> *I met Justine*
> *And said, 'Tell me, neighbour,*
> *What is all this to-do?'*
> *She began to laugh*
> *And then she told me.*
> *She said a fair boy*   *When I heard this,*
> *Had taken our nature*   *I was filled with joy*
> *To pay the ransom*   *And ran to the place*
> *Of every creature.*   *As fast as a partridge.*

The finest ram in the district, a huge bell round its neck, is harnessed to a tiny olive-wood cart decorated with evergreens and red ribbons. Slim arcs of wood form an open canopy to which lighted candles are fixed. A new-born lamb, with its legs lightly bound together, is placed on evergreens in the cart.

A group of children dressed in white, with gold stars on their heads, represent the angels who led the shepherds to the manger on Christmas Eve. They walk before the chief shepherd, who wears a long cloak and leads the ram and the cart, and all the shepherds and shepherdesses follow, carrying lighted tapers. As midnight approaches, they sing:

Shepherds, leave your father's fields
And worship in this mystery
A God supreme in majesty,
Yet clothed in our humanity
And born of a Virgin Mother.

They slowly approach the altar, where the priest waits, holding in his arms an image of the Christ Child. The oldest shepherd takes the lamb from the cart and, bowing low to the priest and to the altar, kisses the foot of the Christ Child. He turns, then bows to the shepherdess standing behind him and hands her the lamb. She repeats the ceremony, which continues along the line of alternate shepherds and shepherdesses until all have offered the lamb to the Christ Child. The procession then re-forms and, led by the musicians, they all sing:

Shepherds of Les Baux,   *Let us sing the Christ Child*
All men of good will   *Who has brought us life,*
Tonight we meet again   *Let us sing the Christ Child.*
In the old chapel.   *Noël has saved us.*

In Yugoslavia oak logs felled before sunrise on December 24th are decorated with red silk, leaves and flowers, and are carried home in candle-lit processions at twilight. As the logs are borne over the threshold, corn or wine is thrown over the first log and it is received into the house with great honour. The housewife scatters straw on the floor and lights a Yule candle which stands in a wheat-sheaf; the head of the house asks a blessing on the home, the occupants, livestock, bees and crops. Then all sit down to a meal. The log is kept burning until morning, when a pig is roasted.

A boy called the *Polaznik* arrives, strews a handful of wheat, saying, 'Christ is born,' to which all reply, 'He is born indeed.' The housewife throws some wheat over the *Polaznik*, who then strikes the burning log, wishing everyone good luck, prosperity and happiness, and he sits on the floor to anchor his wishes to the ground. He is wrapped in a thick blanket which in some way will ensure twelve months' supply of top quality cream. The Slavs also have the custom of going round the orchards commanding the fruit trees to give good harvest, but they also threaten them with a hatchet.

In Czechoslovakia, processions of Moravian children used to carry lighted candles to symbolize the Light that came into the world at Christmas time. In many European countries it was the custom for each member of the congregation to carry a candle to church for the midnight Mass; and at the end of the service, the priest would light the candle of the person nearest to him, who in turn would light his neighbour's, and this would be repeated until everyone present held a lighted candle. They would carry the lighted candles homeward so that the snowy darkness glittered with a galaxy of tiny flames.

Candles lit on Christmas Eve in Norway are extinguished the following morning but are re-lit every evening

until New Year's Day. This custom is also followed in Ireland, where the candles are re-lit and continued until Twelfth Night. As it is considered unlucky to touch the candle once it has been lit the ritual of putting it out is performed by the oldest member of the family.

At one time Swedish festivities started with 'Little Yule' on Saint Lucia's Day, December 13th, when a Saint Lucia Queen or Bride was elected in each village. Originally her name was Lussi or Lussibruden (bride of Lucia), but in the course of time she became identified with the martyred Saint Lucia of Sicily. The chosen girl wore a white dress with a red sash, and a crown of nine lighted candles. She rode out at night with her maids of honour, a horseman and star-boys representing trolls and demons. They visited farms, stables and houses, to bring promise of the return of light and life.

Within the home, the youngest daughter was elected Saint Lucia. She wore the candle-crown to dispense light and she distributed coffee and cinnamon buns whilst Christmas carols were sung. This was followed by a candle-lit breakfast, and extra fodder was provided for the animals. The custom still exists in a modified form.

The longing for light in the long, dark northern winter is apparent in the Swedish carol *Nu tändas tusen Juleljus*:

18

*Now light one thousand Christmas lights
On dark earth here tonight,
One thousand thousand also shine
To make the dark sky bright.*

In honour of the Christ Child's birth-day, a lighted candle is placed in the window of every room in the hope that He will bless the home.

It is the custom in Sweden, as in some parts of Germany, for an unseen person to fling open the door and throw in a gift, or *Julklapp*, wrapped in many layers of paper. On occasion, an old man with a bell and an old woman with a basket of gifts will replace the invisible thrower of *Julklapp*.

A Polish custom on Christmas Eve is to spread hay on the floor and under the tablecloth on which is laid the evening meal, to make the room look like an inn. An *oplatek*, a thin oblong wafer of bread impressed with the Nativity scene, is passed from hand to hand, and each member of the household, beginning with the father, breaks off a piece. An extra place is set at table for Mary and the Christ Child in case they should knock at the door of the 'inn' asking for shelter.

There is a Polish puppet play which tells the story of the Nativity, and for its setting an elaborate church-like construction of gaily coloured turrets and towers is built and carried by the children from house to house. This decorative framework for the Christmas story is called a *szopka*.

In Hungary carol-singers walked in procession to church on Christmas Eve, led by three young girls wearing beautifully embroidered white robes and tall mitres, representing the three Kings who journeyed from the East.

In Russia many of the old Christmas customs have ceased to exist, but the legend of Baboushka will always be remembered. When the Magi journeyed from the East to Bethlehem by the light of the wonderful star, they rested by day. One morning they came to the house of Baboushka and asked her for food and lodging. This she willingly gave, and asked them why they preferred to travel by night. They told her they were going to see the greatest king ever born on earth and were taking him gifts. Baboushka begged to be allowed to go with them, but in a day's time because she must first clean her house and leave it in order for her return. The Magi agreed to her request only if she would leave that same night, in case the star should later disappear. But Baboushka stayed to tidy her house. Then she collected some gifts to take with her, and set out in the hope of catching up with the three Wise Men. But the star had vanished. When finally she reached Bethlehem, Mary, Joseph and the Child had left to escape the wrath of Herod, and Baboushka searches for them to this day. Every year at Christmas time she leaves her home and starts on her travels. When she reaches a house where there is a child she enters quickly, unseen, and then departs, leaving behind a present.

According to Syrian custom, the outer gates of the house are locked on Christmas Eve, a precaution stemming from past persecutions of Christians. A bonfire is built in the centre of the courtyard, around which the entire family stands, holding lighted candles. The youngest member reads the Gospel story of the Nativity and the father lights the bonfire. As the flames rise they sing psalms and make wishes.

In the Syrian church a bonfire is lit in the centre during midnight Mass, while ancient hymns are sung and the

Baboushka

priest carries an image of the Christ Child round the church. After the 'Elevation of the Host' the priest leans over the altar rail and touches the person nearest to him. This is the 'Touch of Peace' and it is passed from one person to the next throughout the whole congregation.

In the seventeenth century the Puritans who sailed to America from England abolished all observation of Christmas, and December 25th in New England was an ordinary working day until the influx of European emigrants in mid-nineteenth century, who took with them their Christmas customs and festivities. Today these customs remain much the same as we know them in England and all other European countries.

The descendants of German settlers in Pennsylvania still celebrate the Feast of Saint Nicholas, whose servant is called *Belsnickel*.

Mexico became Christian after the Spanish conquests. For nine evenings before Christmas the Mexicans enact a *posada*, during which people bearing lighted candles approach a house, sing carols, knock and ask for shelter—which is refused. Then the leader of the procession explains that he is Joseph and indicates Mary, who is accompanying him, whereupon they are immediately invited to enter. Amidst great joy, dancing and feasting take place, followed by fireworks. Children are blindfolded and try to break a suspended jar, *pinata*, which is gaily decorated with coloured paper to represent a bird or a fish. When the jar is broken, sweets, nuts and fruit fall out and everyone rushes to gather up as many as possible.

In New Mexico fires are lit on Christmas Eve outside the houses, and candles in sand-filled paper-bags are put on the roofs and walls, where they make a splendid glow of various colours.

As Christmas in South America coincides with a hot mid-summer, most of the celebrations take place out of doors in the form of fiestas, picnics, fireworks and processions at Midnight Mass.

In the islands of the Caribbean, the Gombey dancers add colour and gaiety to the Christmas festivities. The dancers originated with the African slaves and were first recorded in Bermuda in 1794, when they lasted during the whole of the Christmas octave since the three days' holiday granted to slaves occurred then. Now the dances are performed on Boxing Day and New Year's Day.

Only men take part, dressed in colourful costumes handed down from father to son for many generations. The Captain, once called the Red Devil, wears a long black cloak gaily adorned with ribbons and pieces of mirror, so that you can 'see yourself in the Devil' or 'see behind you'. He carries a whip, to make sure the dancers do not flag, and plays a pipe. The Chiefs wear shorter blue or

(Right) Gombey dancer
(Centre) Buttenmandln and mask, Bavaria (page 13)
(Left) Star-singers of Germany (page 12)

red capes, and the Warriors' capes are shorter still; they carry hatchets, bows and arrows. The whole company wear brief skirts and aprons over brightly coloured fringed trousers. Their head-dresses are made of peacock feathers four feet high. Their faces are masked, though at one time they were painted red or yellow. The dancers promenade round the islands to the incessant rhythm of drums, pausing frequently to perform intricate foot movements and acrobatic leaps.

The most popular drum rhythm is *Greatheart and the Giant*. 'Gombey' is African for a type of drum made from stretched goat-skin and played with the hands or with sticks. The performance is derived partly from the slaves' impression of mummers and partly from African tribal dances and ritual. In the Leeward Island of Nevis the festivity includes the sacrifice of a chicken.

2
Christmas Customs in Britain

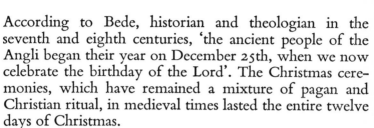

According to Bede, historian and theologian in the seventh and eighth centuries, 'the ancient people of the Angli began their year on December 25th, when we now celebrate the birthday of the Lord'. The Christmas ceremonies, which have remained a mixture of pagan and Christian ritual, in medieval times lasted the entire twelve days of Christmas.

At one time, festoons of holly, ivy, fir, larch and other evergreens were the only form of decoration. The old Welsh carol begins, 'Deck the halls with boughs of holly.' Holly was thought to discourage witches and tax collectors; but made into a wreath it symbolised the crown of thorns, the berries representing the drops of Christ's blood. A wreath of ivy, however, had pagan associations with the crown of Bacchus.

Mistletoe, the sacred plant of the Druids, was at one time, according to Christian legend, a mighty tree, but because it was used for the Cross on which Christ died, it was doomed to become a parasite on other trees. It was considered unlucky to bring holly or even mistletoe into the house before Christmas, and any decorations not removed and burnt by Twelfth Night (that is, the twelfth night after Christmas) are still thought to bring misfortune.

A kissing bush, a large spray of mistletoe, hung from a rafter in the centre of the room, but in Cheshire, Lincolnshire, Northumberland and districts where the plant was rare, a spherical framework was covered with ivy, holly

or evergreens and hung with apples, tiny gifts or ornaments of tin or glass. Candles were set among the foliage and a sprig of mistletoe hung below, a berry being removed for each kiss given beneath it.

In London in the fifteenth century, citizens were ordered to hang lighted lanterns outside their houses. Stow, in his *Survey of London* says: '. . . everyman's house, also their parish churches decked with holme, ivie, bayes and whatsoever the season afforded to be green.' . . . 'At Leadenhall, in Cornhill, a standard of tree, being set up in the midst of the pavement fast in the ground, nailed full of holme and ivie for disport of Christmas to the people . . .' was struck by lightning during a violent storm in 1444.

During the Commonwealth such celebrations were banned, and during the years 1644–1656 Parliament sat on Christmas Day.

Christmas trees originated in the *Paradeisbaum*, the Paradise Tree of German mystery plays. A fir tree hung with apples was ringed round with lighted candles to represent the Garden of Eden. Later, in the fifteenth century, it was decked with white wafers symbolising the Holy Eucharist, and later still, to please the children, gingerbread men, edible angels and figures of Adam and Eve were added. Candles became part of the decorations in the seventeenth century.

The German Christmas tree, the *Tannenbaum*, was introduced into England, according to Greville's *Diary*, by Princess Lieven in 1829. It became popular when the

Prince Consort had a Christmas tree for the royal children at Windsor in 1841. The Victorian tree was decorated with paper cones and tiny metal baskets filled with gilded nuts or sweets, oranges, tinsel stars and tiny lanterns and candles. Originally a model representing the Holy Child adorned the top of the Christmas tree, but in the course of time this became an angel with golden wings, which in turn evolved into the fairy doll with tinsel dress and wand.

In 1850 Charles Dickens referred to 'that pretty German toy, a Christmas tree.' The one he described stood on a table and among other things that he listed as weighing down its branches were miniature tin furniture, paint boxes, needle cases and work boxes, drums, swords and guns, dolls, sugar plum containers in the form of little men with removable heads, fruit covered with gold leaf and humming tops. It was usual to leave the distribution of sweets and fruit until Twelfth Night, thus giving the children something to look forward to and lessening the sorrow of parting with the tree and the Christmas decorations.

The Reverend Francis Kilvert, in his diary for Christmas Eve, 1874, writes: 'In the afternoon I went to Church . . . to put up the Christmas decorations. Dora had been very busy for some days past making the straw letters for the Christmas text . . .' Other helpers '. . . made some pretty ivy knots and bunches for the pulpit panels and the ivy blossoms (sic) cleverly whitened with flour looked just like white flowers.'

Candles, apart from being a source of illumination, symbolised the coming of spring and longer days, and the birth of Christ as the 'Light of the World'. In quite recent times it was usual for chandlers or grocers to make gifts of candles to customers at Christmas.

Parson Woodford in his diary for December 25th, 1790,

recorded: 'I lighted my large Wax-Candle, being Christmas Day, during Tea-time this afternoon for abt an Hour'; and on the same day the following year: 'My large Wax Candle lighted up as usual for one Hour (being Christmas Day) in the Evening.'

Yule logs had to be large enough to fill the entire fireplace and to burn for twelve hours. Faggot bundles were burned in memory of the faggot fire in front of which the Baby Jesus was bathed on the night of His Birth. In Devon, the first person to ignite his bind of faggots under the Yule log would be the first to marry.

Bells are the heralds of Christmas and the New Year, whether they be hand-bells rung by the ringers of Appleton round the Berkshire villages, or great carillons, or simple peals from village churches sounding across the winter fields. At Dewsbury, a single bell tolls for an hour every Christmas Eve, the final stroke sounding exactly at midnight, for 'the Devil died when Christ was born.' This has been done with scarcely a break for seven hundred years, since Sir Thomas Soothill gave the bell, known as 'Black Tom of Soothill,' to atone for the murder of his manservant.

The Reverend Francis Kilvert writes of bells in his diary for 1871: '. . . sat up last night to watch the old year out and the New Year in . . . We opened the dining-room window to "loose in" the sound of the chimes and the New Year, as they say in Wales.' And in Wiltshire on New Year's Eve, 1871, he records: 'At five minutes to midnight the bells of Chippenham Church pealed out loud and clear in the frosty air. We opened a shutter and stood around the window listening. It was a glorious moonlight night.' On New Year's Eve, 1872, he observes: '. . . Langley people always used to say that the Langley Burrell bells rang these words, 'My cow's tail's long, my cow's tail's long.'

At Carlton in Yorkshire, children carry a Vessel (Wassail) cup from house to house, singing a Vessel song:

> *Good Master and Mistress,*
> *While you're sitting by the fire*
> *Pray think of us poor children*
> *Who are wandering in the mire.*

The Vessel cup is a cardboard box, decorated with scraps of ribbon and material, containing a small doll which in former times was probably an image of the Christ Child.

In some northern districts children begging money take round a Milly box lined with sugar and sweets. The word Milly probably originated in 'My Lady', and the two dolls in the box may formerly have been statuettes of the Virgin and Child.

The Mari Lwyd (Holy Mary) mummers of Llangynwyd, Glamorganshire, sing traditional rhymes. The chief mummer wears a skeleton horse's head decorated with coloured ribbons and streamers. His smock is a survival of a shroud or animal skin. As a reminder of past battles and enmity, householders at first refuse the mummers admittance, but finally they are asked in and entertained.

In Andover, Hampshire, on Christmas Eve, Christmas Day and Boxing Day, mummers festooned with paper streamers mime a medieval interpretation of death and resurrection. A similar theme is enacted at Mashfield in Gloucestershire, but with the addition of singing and dancing.

Originally performed at Christmas, the New Year and Twelfth Night, the Horn Dance of Abbots Bromley probably symbolises the right of local people centuries ago to hunt reindeer and wild boars in the forests which covered large areas of Staffordshire. It remains basically the same as when first danced in the time of Henry III.

Twelve dancers take part, six of whom wear Tudor
costume and carry reindeer antlers mounted on short
poles. The other six are Robin Hood riding a hobby horse,
Maid Marion, a medieval entertainer, a boy with a crossbow and arrow and two musicians who supply the accompaniment to the dance on concertina and triangle, assisted
by the boy banging the crossbow with the arrow and by
the hobby horse clapping its wooden jaws together.

In Lincolnshire the Hood Game is played on the church
green at Haxey on Twelfth Night. It starts with the Fool
making a speech, only to be shouted down by the crowd.
This leads to 'smoking the Fool,' which is done by lighting
paper near him and smoking him out. The Hood, a leather
roll twenty-two feet long, is thrown to the crowd. Some
try to push it into one Haxey inn whilst others endeavour
to push it into a rival hostelry. The Hood is retained by
the successful 'goal' for twelve months and the victors
are rewarded with free drinks. The Lord and eleven
Boggins supervise the boisterous struggle for the Hood,
and these twelve characters and the Fool wear traditional
costume. The origin of the game is said to be in the
thirteenth century, when Lady de Mowbray, whilst out

riding, lost her red hood which it took thirteen labourers to chase and retrieve.

In many parts of early nineteenth-century Wales, Christmas Day was the occasion for a boisterous game of football, all active inhabitants—men, women and children —taking part. The opposing sides were hamlet against hamlet, the hillmen, supposedly of part Irish descent, against the lowlanders, who were considered to be of pure Welsh stock. The football was usually made by the shoemaker from a bladder and the aim was to get it by fair means or foul back to one of the hamlets. The game commenced after morning service and for at least twenty minutes the football was lost to view in a flailing mass of humanity. When it had been extricated and hours later taken to one of the hamlets, the victory was proclaimed with shouting and firing guns. There were many casualties, for the contest was fought with great violence and often bitterness, which owed much to ancient clan animosity.

Rituals dating back to barbaric sacrificial rites in honour of a Viking god or to celebrate the return of the sun are still carried out at Lerwick in Shetland. 'Up Helly Aa' was originally associated with Yule celebrations and now takes the form of a torchlight procession of 'Vikings' marching to the town square, where a Viking ship is set on fire to the chanting of an Up Helly Aa song. As with so many Nordic customs, there is strong emphasis on light, representing the return of life to the world after months of cold and darkness.

Overton, Hampshire, has a famous mummers' play, including the characters of Father Christmas, King George or Saint George, Turkish Knight, Bold Slasher, Quack Doctor and Twing Twang. The ancient morality plays were forerunners of such entertainments.

In many parts of Britain it was traditional for choristers and scholars to elect one of their number to act as Bishop

31

from December 6th, Saint Nicholas's Day, to December 28th, the Day of Holy Innocents. He wore episcopal vestments during this period and celebrated all but the most sacred services. If he died whilst in office, he was buried with full honours appropriate to his rank. There is a monument to a Boy Bishop in Salisbury Cathedral. The Bishop led processions through the streets, collecting alms for the poor, a custom observed from the ninth century until the reign of Henry VIII; it was recommenced under the reign of Mary and abolished by Elizabeth I. It has recently been revived at Berden in Hertfordshire, Marske in Yorkshire, and at Rye and Walsingham.

The Lord of Misrule or, in Scotland, the Abbot of Unreason, was elected for the duration of the Christmas revels and sometimes combined this with the office of Boy Bishop. He had his own court and attendants, often his own pillory, stocks and gibbet. His word was law, as shown in the carol of 1500:

> *Make we merry, both more and less*
> *For now is the time of Christmas.*
> *Let no man come into this hall,*
> *Nor groom, nor page, nor yet marshall,*

If that he say he cannot sing.
  Some other sport then let him bring,
That it may please at this feasting.
  If he say he naught can do,
Then for my love, ask him no mo',
  But to the stocks then let him go.

The sixteenth-century writer John Stow recounts how every great household from the King's Court downwards was given over to the Lord of Misrule and his followers (who could number anything from twenty to one hundred persons) for at least twelve days ending at Candlemas, 'In all which space there were fine and subtil disguisinges, masks and mummeries, with playinge at cards for counters . . .' all 'contending, without quarrel or offence, who shoulde make the rarest pastimes to delight behoulders.'

In 1583, in *The Anatomie of Abuses*, P. Stubbes described the procession to church, headed by the Lord of Misrule and supplemented by dragons and hobby horses, 'their pypers pyping, their drummers thundering, their stumpes dancing, their belles jyngling . . . like madde men.'

These festivities were very expensive for the patron, and in 1490 Henry VII paid £32 18s 6½d—a large sum in those days—for all the pageantry and entertainment organized by his Lord of Misrule.

It is from these ceremonies that some of our surnames derive. A Boy Bishop or an Abbot of Unreason would retain the name Bishop or Abbot after his period of office was over, whilst those who had represented the Magi continued to be known as King or Rex.

Peculiar to the Fen country were the 'Molly Dancers (perhaps originally 'My Lady' dancers), who performed in private houses, farms and public houses, accompanied by musicians playing the dulcimer, fiddle or concertina.

Characters in mummer's plays, including Robin Hood on hobby horse (page 30) and a straw bear (see below)

They were all country labourers in fancy dress, and in lieu of payment they received hot mulled drinks. They started by dancing on Christmas Eve only, but, finding their entertainment popular, they later performed on several days until the whole district had been visited.

A rival form of rural entertainment in the Fen country was a group of men leading another man covered entirely in straw to represent a straw bear. They, too, visited public houses and homes at Christmas time to enact a short play. The bear would take part, dancing on all fours and singing. Sometimes these mummers did not appear until Plough Monday, the first Monday after Epiphany, to celebrate the start of the ploughing season.

December 27th used to be called 'Gooding Day.' On this day needy old women made themselves as presentable as possible and called on the wealthier families in the district, or on past employers, and even on their more prosperous friends. By tradition, they were given food and scraps left over from the Christmas celebrations, though later this form of charity was superseded by gifts of money or groceries.

The Morris dancers of Brampton, Oxfordshire, blacken their faces to represent Moors. At Grenoside near Sheffield clog and sword dancers entertain at Christmas, the widow of each deceased dancer receiving half-a-crown from the collection made after the performance.

Burning the ash faggot is a Christmas tradition at Dunster, Somerset. The ash is the only green wood that will burn.

In Gloucestershire, farmers light dawn fires in their fields at the New Year. There are thirteen fires: one for Our Lord and twelve smaller fires for the Apostles, the one for Judas being stamped out immediately. The celebration ends with plum cake and cider.

At Bredwardine-on-the-Wye, Herefordshire, the Reverend Francis Kilvert noted on New Year's Eve, 1877:

'After I had gone to bed, I saw from where I lay a bright blaze sprung up in the field beyond the river, and I knew at once that they were keeping up the old custom of Burning the Bush on New Year's Day in the morning . . . the whole Valley can be seen early on New Year's Morning alight with fires Burning the Bush . . .'

The Reverend Giles Moore of Horstead Keynes in Sussex writing in his diary during the years 1655–1679 records that on December 26th, 'I gave the howling boys 6d.' This was part of the ceremony of Apple-howling in which a troop of boys went from orchard to orchard, encircling the trees and chanting:

> Stand fast, root, bear well, top
> Pray the God send us a good howling crop.
> Every twig, apples big,
> Every bough, apples enou;
> Hats full, caps full,
> Full quarters, sacks full.

They rapped the trees with their sticks and one boy blew on a cow's horn.

Herrick in *Hesperides* also comments on the custom:

> Wassail the trees that they may beare
> You many a plum, and many a peare:
> For more or less fruits they will bring,
> As you do give the wassailing.

On old Twelfth Night, January 17th, at Carhampton in Somerset there was also a ceremony of wassailing the trees. At dusk villagers formed a ring round the largest apple tree. Guns were fired between the branches to frighten away evil spirits endangering the crop, the trunk was splashed with cider and toast and cake soaked in cider was left on the branches as a thank offering. The proceedings terminated with a toast and the chant:

Old apple tree, old apple tree,
We've come to wassail thee.

An old custom in Herefordshire was to take a wassail bowl into the byre and to drink to the health of the animals. A crown cake, with a hole in the centre, was hung on the horn of an ox and if it was tossed off it meant good luck for the owners.

At Ackworth in Yorkshire, a small sheaf of grain for the birds is hung round the neck of Saint Cuthbert's

statue in the sanctuary porch of the parish church on Christmas Day. It is an old custom originating in Scandinavia. But in Bury St Edmunds, Suffolk, owls and red squirrels were less fortunate, as it was customary to hunt them on Christmas Day.

In Wales, in the last century, the minister was escorted from his house to the four o'clock service on Christmas morning by young men with lighted torches. The service, lasting until daybreak, was called Plygain or The Crowing of the Cock.

An interesting extract from Pepys' diary, dated December 24th, 1667, reads: 'By coach to St James's, it being about six at night: my design being to see the ceremonies this night being the eve of Christmas at the

Queen's chapel. I got in almost up to the rail, and with a great deal of patience stood until nine at night to two in the morning in a very great crowd . . .' His disappointment is expressed in the words 'there being nothing but a high masse.' He had expected 'to have had a child born and dressed there and a great deal of do . . .'

3

Christmas Entertainments

In addition to religious processions, entertainment on a grand scale has been part of Christmas throughout the ages. The mummers' play was popular in Great Britain in the fifteenth and eighteenth centuries. Masked persons paraded the streets and ended by presenting a play, usually representing a fight in which a champion is killed and revived by a doctor.

At Court there were banquets and masked balls, which

in the seventeenth century were very elaborate indeed. In Georgian times balls were held in the Assembly Rooms and were attended only by a small community.

Since Cromwell's time play-going had become part of the seasonal festivities, reaching its peak with the nineteenth-century pantomimes, flying ballets, spectacular transformation scenes, and the traditional finale, the Harlequinade, which originated with the Italian Comedy or *Comedia dell'Arte*. In the sixteenth century Italian companies of comedians travelled across Europe, improvising amusing character sketches from which emerged stock characters, always played by the actor who created or developed the rôle. Some were comic, some straight characters; they included Harlequin, Pantaloon, Scaramouche, Pulcinella (the forerunner of Punch) and Pedrolino or Pierrot (see page 40). Some of these characters later became the leading rôles in London's Drury Lane pantomimes under Mr Rich in the early eighteenth century.

Some Christmas plays, such as *Peter Pan* and *Where the Rainbow Ends*, were written solely for children. The Pollock Toy Theatres, with the Penny Plain and Tuppence Coloured Drama sheets, were a joy to all ages.

The Victorians and Edwardians enjoyed charades and the more sophisticated tableaux vivants, the latter being groups of people dressed and posed to represent historical or religious events, famous paintings or allegorical subjects. Often considerable expense and time were spent on these amateur productions, much favoured by wealthy people and royalty.

Other entertainments at Christmas were folk and country dances, such games as bob-apple, blind man's buff and bran tubs with their numerous surprises. 'A great game of snap-dragon' pleased Mr Pickwick and past generations: 'and when fingers enough were burned with that, and all the raisins were gone . . .' they sat roasting chestnuts and telling ghost stories.

One of the great amusements for children is to see what Santa Claus has put into their Christmas stockings. At one time there was always an orange in the toe, and then there were small items such as whistles, sheets of picture scraps, packets of coloured beads, balls of Berlin wool for making reins or working texts, apples, sweets and pink sugar mice; but today the stockings are often filled with much more expensive gifts.

Christmas gift wrappings have become more elaborate than the original coloured tissue papers. Now gaily coloured paper and plastic, variously designed by artists, wrap the parcels, which are tied with coloured tinsel and ribbons to add to their beauty.

Streets are festooned with elaborate decorations, costing millions of pounds, and multi-coloured electric lights obliterating the sky. Non-stop amplified carols replace the Angels' voices, and the electric star is a substitute for the Star of Bethlehem.

In these days vast numbers of Christmas trees invade the towns and cities, the churches, cathedrals, homes and town

squares. A large tree is to be found in Trafalgar Square, London, which is sent from Norway every year in gratitude for the liberation of that country in the Second World War.

The custom of sending out Christmas cards to absent friends and relatives is little over one hundred years old. It started in England in 1843, when Sir Henry Cole, founder of the Victoria and Albert Museum and organizer of the Great Exhibition of 1851, commissioned F. C. Horsley, R.A., to design a Christmas card for him for sale in Cole's art shop in Old Bond Street, London. Within a rustic frame, it depicted a family enjoying a festive meal, and in side panels showed food and clothing being distributed to the poor. Another card, similar in approach, with Gothic motifs, was designed in 1848 by William Maw Egley, a sixteen-year-old engraver.

The public showed little interest in the idea of cards until the 1860s, when well-known stationers such as Raphael Tuck, de la Rue and Marcus Ward developed it. This time it became a success both in Great Britain and abroad, especially in America. Few designs were of a religious nature, many were comic. In the late 1860s Kate Greenaway's cards were greatly in demand. Robins were featured on cards as bearers of Christmas greetings because at one time Victorian postmen wore red uniforms and were nicknamed robin redbreasts.

Later Christmas cards were very elaborate, with glitter and frosting, real and paper lace, and with ribbon and tassel fastening them. Some opened out to reveal angels, flowers, bells, echoing the transformation scenes so fashionable in theatres and pantomimes of the period. Religious themes began to take their place, in addition to coaching scenes, robins, glowing firesides and landscapes of a way of life already being replaced by steam and the industrial Victorian age. In the present day greeting

43

cards have become a world-wide major commercial business.

Carols are another very popular form of Christmas entertainment. The word 'carol' is probably derived from the Greek *khoraules* (chorus). The earliest carols were sung by the dancers taking part in a chorus or circling dance.

The monks and priests in Italy sang hymns in celebration of the Nativity from the fifth century onwards; but it was not until the thirteenth century that Saint Francis encouraged songs of praise to be written in which the entire congregation could join.

The singing of carols became a feature of Christmas throughout the whole of Europe. Carols were also sung by minstrels in baronial halls and they were popularised when they were introduced into the medieval Mystery plays performed in many cities at Christmas and other religious festivals.

The York, Chester, Towneley and Coventry plays were particularly famous and in some instances are still performed at Christmas. These plays evolved from simple Biblical events reconstructed by priests in front of the high altar, and developed into more ambitious efforts that included laymen in the cast. Later they were enacted out of doors with the cathedral as a backdrop and finally on a raised platform with trapdoors and other devices to achieve miraculous effects. The productions became elaborate and covered a range of religious and sometimes mythological subjects, from the Creation, the Garden of Eden, Noah, Daniel, the life of Christ, to a highly dramatic representation of Heaven and the mouth of Hell. The shepherds, the demons and Satan were accepted as comic characters. Sometimes the various Guilds were each responsible for a separate tableau. The shipwrights portrayed Noah, the tailors Adam and Eve and the carpenters Joseph and Mary; and they were mounted on carts pulled by four horses or oxen and passed in procession before the audience in the town square.

In 1546 Queen Margaret heard the *Coventry Carol* when the Shearmen and Tailors' Company of that city produced their pageant, the carol being sung by the women of Bethlehem before the arrival of Herod's soldiers to slay their children. It has been handed down through the centuries by mummers and rhymers at Christmas time.

In past centuries people sang carols as they danced round the crib in the church, just as today the Swedes sing carols while dancing round the Christmas tree. Until recent times boys danced before the altar in Seville Cathedral to music provided by flutes, castanets and other musical instruments.

The Tudors and Stuarts introduced carols into the Court masques, but these were suppressed by Cromwell.

In 1764, Parson James Woodford recorded in his diary: 'New singers came very late this evening and they sung a Christmas Carol and an Anthem, and they had cyder as usual and two shillings.' Four years later he wrote: 'It being Christmas Eve, we had the New Singers of Castle Cary this evening at the Parsonage, and they having been at great expenses in learning to sing, my father and myself gave them double what we used to do, and therefore instead of one shilling we gave 0.2.0.'

The following year the singers were in disgrace. 'To Cary Singers, this evening being Xmas Eve, at Parsonage, after giving them a lecture concerning their late behaviour in Church, on promise of amendment gave 0.2.0.'

At Thaxted, Essex, on the morning of Boxing Day, the Feasts of Saint Stephen and Saint Wenceslas, an ancient Cornish carol is sung, called *The Dancing Day*, commemorating the life, death and resurrection and ascension of Our Lord. It has eleven verses in all, the first three as follows:

Tomorrow shall be my dancing day:
I would my true love did so chance
To see the legend of my play,
To call my true love to my dance.

Then was I born of a virgin pure,
Of her I took fleshly substance,
Thus was I knit to man's nature
To call my true love to my dance.

In a manger laid and wrapped I was
So very poor, this was my chance,
Betwixt an ox and a silly poor ass,
To call my true love to my dance.

Carols vary in subject matter from sacred to secular, from legend—*Good King Wenceslas*—to a late eighteenth-century memory test—*The Twelve Days of Christmas*—or its French counterpart *La Foi du Roi*, which perhaps not surprisingly is devoted to food. The singers of carols and the settings in which they are sung are similarly diverse, from the juvenile waits on the doorstep to the carols by candlelight in King's College Chapel, Cambridge.

In 1223 Pope Honorius III granted Saint Francis of Assisi in Italy permission to reconstruct the Nativity scene in a cave so that the people could visualize the wonder of the first Christmas and sing carols in honour of the Christ Child. In Austria and Germany, *Kindelwiegen* or cradle-rocking is still part of a carol service.

There are valleys in the Austrian Tirol known as the Valleys of Music and Song, where the inhabitants were once noted as repairers of musical instruments. In the village of Arnsdorf near Salzburg the carol *Stille Nacht (Silent Night)* originated. For years the manuscript lay forgotten in an organ, but it was discovered when the instrument was being repaired and was first sung in 1818.

47

4

Christmas Legends and Beliefs

King Wenceslas

The story of this tenth-century Duke of Bohemia, canonized after he was murdered by his brother Boleslav I, is told in the carol *Good King Wenceslas*. Although the night was bitterly cold, the air around the king was as warm as on a summer evening, and where he trod the snow melted so that his page could follow in his footsteps.

Shemuel

When the angel appeared to the shepherds, they all hastened to the stable, with the exception of Shemuel. There was a sick man, a stranger, in their camp, and Shemuel stayed to nurse him. The shepherds returned, full of the glorious things they had seen. Shemuel was very sad to have missed these wonders and decided he would go the following night. However, by that time the stranger had died and Shemuel himself was very ill. He and the other shepherds took this as a sign that he was unworthy to witness the marvels in Bethlehem, and he was ashamed.

As he lay dying, a great light shone out of heaven, and, looking up, Shemuel saw the Trinity seated majestically on high. All his misery left him as he realized that this vision was to compensate him for his self-sacrifice the previous night. He died in great happiness and his soul was borne to Paradise by angels.

The Glow-worm

At one time the glow-worm was just a tiny brown beetle with no distinguishing glow of light. On the first Christmas she heard the angels' message and saw the shepherds running through her field on the way to the manger. She decided  that she, too, must go and take with her her only treasure, a seed saved when the farmer cut the hay.

She was a long while reaching the stable, pushing her hay-seed before her through the tall grass. When eventually she did arrive she was so insignificant that nobody noticed her, except the Child Jesus. He saw her, smiled and touched her with His finger, and ever since she has glowed with a little ray from His halo, so that she can guide pilgrims on their way.

The Miraculous Stag

In Hungarian legend, there is a stag on whose horn-tips burn a hundred thousand candles. 'They burn without being lit: they go out of themselves,' says the carol.

The Beasts

In a twelfth-century English carol the donkey carried Mary to the stable in Bethlehem and then the other beasts contributed to the comfort of the newly born Child.

The cow gave her manger for a bed and hay for a pillow, and warmed the Child with her breath, which

ever since has been sweeter than that of other animals. The sheep gave wool for a blanket and the doves cooed Him to sleep. The ox stood patiently by, symbolizing those who bear a yoke silently whilst labouring for the good of others.

The Glastonbury Thorn

Saint Joseph of Arimathea came to Glastonbury in the thirteenth century and planted his staff on Weary-all Hill, where it grew into a thorn tree which flowers at Christmas. The original tree was destroyed by order of Cromwell, but cuttings had been taken and replanted. It is first mentioned in a poem of 1502.

The Daisy

The daisy was the only gift the youngest shepherd could bring to the manger. The Christ Child kissed it and the tips of its petals have been rosy ever since.

The Holly

The hollybush stood at the stable door, but it was without berries as the birds had eaten them. In honour of the Nativity the holly produced buds, flowers and scarlet berries, all in the space of the one Holy Night.

The Christmas Rose

A little girl of Bethlehem crept to the stable door to peep

at Mary and her Baby. She wished to give Him a present, but her parents were poor and she had no money, so she decided to give Him a flower. She searched all day, but the hills and fields around Bethlehem were winter-black and patched with snow.

The girl returned, weeping, but as she passed the stable a ray of light from within shone on a clump of pure white flowers, which certainly had not been growing there in the morning. She gathered a bunch and took them to the Baby: they were the first Christmas roses to bloom on earth.

The Fire Flower

On Christmas Eve, the people of Cuernavaca in Mexico attended Mass in their cathedral, taking with them gifts for the Christ Child. Outside stood a little peasant girl, too poor to afford a present, but an angel appeared, instructing her to gather the tall wayside weeds. As she carried these into the great cathedral, the topmost leaves on each stem appeared to burst into flame, and thereafter the plant was known as the *flor de fuego* or *flor de la Noehebuena*—the fire flower of the Holy Night: the poinsettia.

The Bees

Ever since the first Christmas Eve, the bees have hummed the hundredth Psalm in their hive at midnight. At this hour, all the beasts of creation kneel facing the East, and for a short time have the gift of human speech. Great misfortune overtakes anyone foolish enough to listen to their conversation.

The Cock

The cock in the stableyard behind the inn at Bethlehem was the first creature to proclaim the birth of Christ, crying, *Christus natus est*—'Christ is born'.

When the Magi, on their way to Bethlehem, appeared before Herod and told him that the greatest king of all was lying in a stable, he refused to believe them.

'If this is true,' said Herod, 'then the roasted cock in this silver dish will arise and crow three times.'

Instantly the cock arose and thrice proclaimed, *Christus natus est*.

This legend is recorded in the ballad-carol *King Herod and the Cock*, dating from the early thirteenth century:

> *'If this be true,' King Herod said,*
> *'As thou hast told to me,*
> *This roasted cock that lies in the dish*
> *Shall crow full fences three.'*

> *The cock soon thrustened, and feathered well,*
> *By the work of God's own hand,*
> *And he did crow full fences three*
> *In the dish where he did stand.*

The Robin

A robin was sheltering in the stable rafters the night that Christ was born. The angels and the shepherds, filled with wonder, were praising God, and the robin sang with joy. It was the first bird song the Child had ever heard and He rewarded the robin by making his voice sweeter still. Ever since that night the robin has sung his best on Christ's birthday.

The Crow and the Crane

An ancient carol tells how, after the Nativity, a crow and a crane were discussing the miraculous event.

The carnal (the crow) asks the crane:

Where is the golden cradle
That Christ was rocke'd in?
Where are the silken sheets
That Jesus was wrapped in?

The crane replies:

A manger was the cradle
That Christ was rocked in:
The provender the asses left,
So sweetly he slept on.

The Wren

The wren is no doubt connected with Christmas because it braves the winter of northern climes and fills the air with its resonant and vigorous song. But it was not a happy time for wrens.

The French name for wren was *troglodyte*, a cave dweller, also *père de la bécasse*, father of the woodcock. It was even thought to be the offspring of the polecat, able to fly to great heights, launching itself from the back of an eagle.

In Suffolk wrens were hunted on Boxing Day, and in the Isle of Man a wren was caught, killed, placed on a bier and then carried to church whilst solemn dirges were sung and a knell was tolled. Another Manx custom in-

53

volved a caged wren; but now a bunch of feathers is substituted for the bird, which is enclosed in a hoop decorated with ribbons and evergreens, and the local carol or folk song is sung.

Ireland also has its wren ceremonies on Boxing Day, or Saint Stephen's Day as it is known there. Wrens were hunted by boys and girls wearing masks and fancy dress. They called on all their neighbours, singing:

> *The wren, the wren, the king of all birds,*
> *On St Stephen's Day was caught in the furze.*
> *We got him there, as you may see.*
> *And put him up on the Holly Tree.*

> Chorus:
> *Hurrah! me boys. Hurrah! Hurrah! me boys, Hurrah!*
> *Knock at the knocker, and ring at the bell,*
> *Give us a copper for singin' so well;*
> *Singin' so well, singin' so well,*
> *Give us a copper for singin' so well.*

They were given food and drink, and money to be used for charitable purposes.

Wren-hunting was also known in France. Sonnini, writing at the end of the eighteenth century, says that in late December a band of men and boys from Le Ciotat, near Marseilles, armed with swords and pistols, went wren-hunting and, to ensure success, took a captive bird with them. A wren was brought back hanging from a stout pole carried by two men and paraded as though it were a great burden. It was weighed on a huge pair of scales in a ceremonious fashion, and then the company sat down to a feast.

In Carcassonne, at the close of the year, boys beat the bushes in search of wrens. The first to kill one was proclaimed 'King' and he carried the wren back on a pole. The festivities lasted for days and on the last night the king led a fife-and-drum torchlight procession and chalked '*Vive le roi*' and the date of the year on street doors. On Twelfth Day the king went to High Mass robed in blue, with crown and sceptre, preceded by a man carrying the wren on a pole decorated with oak, olive branches and mistletoe. Later the king waited on the Bishop, the Mayor and important citizens, collecting money for general feasting and merry-making.

If the men of Mirabeau failed to catch the first wren and a woman succeeded in doing so, she was entitled to chase the men and blacken their faces with soot and mud. It was traditional to bury the wren in the churchyard on Twelfth Night with full ceremony.

The captured bird fared better at Entraigues: it was released by the priest at Midnight Mass on Christmas Eve, with a pink ribbon tied to its leg, possibly to show that it should not be caught again.

In some countries there is the legend that the wren brought moss and feathers for a coverlet for the Christ Child. Wren feathers are therefore considered particularly lucky.

5

Christmas Fare

Although it is recognized that most people eat more at Christmas time than at any other feast-day in the year, our appetites seem small when our Christmas fare is compared with the gargantuan feasts of our forefathers, which lasted for hours and even days, accompanied by song and ceremony.

In Norse mythology, Freyr, the god of peace and plenty, used to ride on a boar, and as his festival came at Yule a boar was always sacrificed in his honour. The custom spread to other countries until the boar's head took pride of place at Christmas feasts throughout Europe, being carried in procession to the accompaniment of drums, trumpets or carols.

> *The boris hed in hondes I brynge,*
> *With garlondes gay and byrdes syngynge;*

and the 'byrdes syngynge' could well have been live birds as in the celebrated *Sing a Song of Sixpence* pie.

Directions for serving the boar's head are given in the seventeenth-century William King's *Art of Cookery*:

. . . . send up the Brawner's Head,
Sweet Rosemary and Bays around it spread:
His foaming tusks let some large Pippin grace,
Or 'midst these thund'ring Spears an Orange place.

A traditional English carol also mentions a boar's head 'bedeck'd with bays and rosemary', and this custom survives in the ceremony at New College, Oxford, where, surrounded by small banners, an orange in its jaw and wreathed in sprays of gilded rosemary, holly, laurel and bayleaf, the boar's head is borne on a silver dish by serving men. Behind them walk a herald and singers in procession. The provost presents the chief singer with the orange and the guests with the sprays of rosemary and bayleaf. The accompanying carol includes the words, '. . . our steward hath provided this, in honour of the King of Bliss.' The custom is said to commemorate a student who disturbed a boar in Shotover Forest, thrusting a copy of Aristotle down its throat and escaping unharmed.

Christmas puddings were originally a stiffened form of plum porridge made from meatbroth, raisins, wine, fruit juices, spices and brown bread.

Mince pies, at the end of the sixteenth century, contained mutton, neats' tongue, fruit, chicken, eggs and spices.

Turkey first appeared in Europe in the sixteenth century, brought from Mexico by the Spanish conquerors. Before that, swans, bustards and peacocks with gilded beaks and elaborately garnished with their own feathers were the Christmas poultry; and in the nineteenth century goose was extremely popular.

Baddeley cake takes its name from Robert Baddeley, a chef who became an actor. When he died in 1794 he left one hundred pounds to pay for wine and cake for the company playing at the Theatre Royal in Drury Lane, London, on Twelfth Night.

Goose and turkey (see below),
and heron (page 61)

Yule spice cakes are a Yorkshire speciality. In Yorkshire, too, it is the custom to spread brandy butter on Christmas pudding. There is a record of a splendid Christmas pie made in Yorkshire, which contained pigeon, poultry, fowl, goose, turkey, ham, woodcock and moor fowl. Four pounds of butter went into the pie and six pounds into the crust, together with a bushel of flour, a dozen eggs and two pounds of suet.

Another gargantuan pie, recorded by Hone in his *Table Book* of 1770, contained four geese, two turkeys, four wild ducks, two rabbits, two curlews, seven blackbirds, six pigeons, four partridges, six snipe, two woodcock, two neats' tongues; two bushels of flour and twenty pounds of butter went to make the pastry.

H. and M. Misson recorded at the end of the seventeenth century: 'Every family against Christmas makes a famous Pye, which they call Christmas Pye; it is a great nostrum the composition of this pasty: it is a most learned mixture of neats' tongues, chicken, eggs, sugar, raisins, lemon and orange peel, various kinds of spicery, etc. They also make a sort of soup with plums, which is not at all inferior to the Pye, which is in their language call'd Plum-Porridge.'

Hyul-doos or Yule Doos, made in Durham and Northumberland, are pastry figures with currant buttons down the front. Saffron and currant cakes made in Cornwall are tokens of good will.

Cassava pie is always served in Bermuda with the main Christmas meal. It is made from grated cassava root, a dozen eggs and a pound and a half of fresh pork, a small fowl, butter, brown sugar and nutmeg. It can be eaten hot or cold, and the aim is to have as large as pie as possible. The crust resembles semolina pudding in texture. The pie apparently derives from slave days, when negroes were permitted to grow their own cassava. As they ate it on Boxing Day, it would appear that the meat consisted of scraps left over from their master's Christmas dinner.

Twelfth Night or Bean cake is customary in France, Germany, Holland and England. It is a rich iced cake, decorated with flowers, gold and silver stars, dragons, the Three Kings and other decorations. Baked in it are a bean and a pea, and the finders of these become King and Queen for Twelfth Night. Sometimes a button symbolizing a bachelor, a thimble signifying a seamstress and a ring for marriage are added. In France two portions of the cake are set aside for God and Our Lady.

The Reverend Henry Teonge spent Christmas in 1675 on board ship and recorded: 'Chrismas day wee keepe thus. At 4 in the morning our trumpeters all doe flatt their trumpets . . . playing a levite at each cabine door . . . wishing a merry Chrismas . . . Our Captaine had all his officers and gentlemen to dinner with him, where he had excellent good fayre: a rib of beife, plumb-puddings, minct pyes and plenty of good wines of severall sorts . . .'

Timothy Burrell of Ockenden House, Cuckfield, in Sussex was a barrister-at-law and kept a journal-account book illustrated by little marginal sketches of the items and events recorded: livestock, farm implements and household things, such as candles, spoons, etc.

It was his custom to invite a number of less well-off people to dine with him at Christmas time, a practice he followed for twenty-six years.

In 1706 they partook of 'Plumm pottage, calves head and bacon, goose, pig, plumm pottage, roast beef, sirloin, veale, a loin, goose, plumm pottage, boiled beef, a clod, two baked puddings, three dishes of minced pies, two capons, two dishes of tarts, two pullets.'

The following day, January 2nd, 1706 he provided 'Plumm pottage, boiled leg of mutton, goose, pig, plumm pottage, roast beef, veal, roasted pig, plumm pottage, boiled beef, a rump, two baked puddings, three dishes of minced pies, two capons, two dishes of tarts, two pullets.' The plumm pottage which recurs between courses was in the nature of a broth, sometimes called plumm broth.

Between the years 1759 and 1793, Parson James Woodford recorded various Christmas repasts: cheese, rabbit and port at New College, Oxford, in 1759; 'Rump beef of thirty pound roasted and three large plum puddings,' in Somerset in 1764. Back at Oxford in 1773, his Christmas dinner, shared by fourteen Senior Fellows, comprised of 'two fine Codds boiled with fryed Souls round them and oyster sauce, a fine sirloin of Beef roasted, some peas, soup and an orange Pudding for the first course; for the second we had a lease of Wild Duck roasted, a fore Qu. of Lamb and sallad and mince pies . . . After the second course there was a fine plumb cake.' And, as usual, there were rabbits for supper. Roast beef, plum pudding, mince-pies, roast fowls, boiled rabbit and onion sauce, good punch and strong beer, made up the other Christmas dinners he shared with his aged parishioners.

The boiled beef eaten by the Anglo-Saxons at Christmas

had been killed, dried and salted in November. Geese, chickens and mutton cooked on a spit were offered, thus impaled, to each guest, so that he could cut a hunk for himself. Frumenty, a pudding made from wheat, milk, spice and honey, and oat cakes, formed the second course. A vast supply of mead and cider was consumed. The hot spiced ale, in which floated roasted apples, filled a huge wassail bowl. They drank from horns, wooden cups or footless glasses which, as they could not stand, had to be drained at one draught. Morat made from honey and mulberries, and pigment from wine, spices and honey were favourite liqueurs of the time.

In the reign of Henry V, a royal banquet contained three huge courses, one of which included many varieties of fish and sea food such as turbot, sturgeon, carp, porpoise, crayfish, whelks, prawns and eels. Richard II 'kept a most Royal Christmas in his newly built Westminster Hall, with daily jousting and runnings at the tilt, whereunto resorted such a number of people that there was every day spent twenty-eight or twenty-six oxen, and three hundred sheep, besides fowls without number.'

In the fifteenth century, feasts consisted of three courses, each containing a large variety of dishes ranging from boar's head (viand royal), herons, cygnets, pheasants, roast porpoise and salmon, to venison in frumenty, bitterns, peacocks and cranes in the second course. The final course gave a choice of quail, curlew and egret, also dillegrout which was concocted from capon, spices, almond milk and sugar.

Special drinks were hippocras, a spiced wine cordial, clarrie (later claret), which was mead and honey mixed with spiced red wine, and garhiofilue, made from honey, white wine and cloves. Ale and cider were also served.

'Now Capons, and Hennes, besides Turkies, Geese and Duckes, besides Beefe and Mutton, must all die for the

great Feast, for in twelve days a multitude of people will not bee fed with a little: now plummes and spice, sugar and honey, square it among pies and broth . . .' wrote Nicholas Breton in the late sixteenth century.

Roast beef and Christmas goose were popular with the Tudors. Each of the meal's three courses could run to over thirty dishes. Neats' tongues, haunch of venison, swan, turkey, pies of finely chopped meat, called chewets, a kid stuffed with pudding, salads, custards, olive pie and fricassées were much favoured. These would be followed by sturgeons, shrimps, salmon smelts and lobster; also woodcock and snipe or lark pie.

Christmas pie and plum porridge, syllabubs, jellies and mince pies were among the sweets. Popular drinks were cherry brandy, sack posset, or a wassail bowl filled with 'lambs' wool' (spiced ale).

The presentation of some of these dishes was elaborate and spectacular, incorporating cannon and live birds. Between courses of a fifteenth-century banquet, a fantastic confection of sugar and wax, called a solty or soltelte, was set in the centre of the table. It was demolished to reveal gifts and tokens for the company.

Mulled ale, beer or elderberry wine are warming Christmas drinks, but the most traditional are punch or the wassail bowl. Punch was made from sugar, Rhenish wine, water, lime and lemon juice, ambergris, musk, brandy and nutmeg, according to a seventeenth-century recipe; though an early nineteenth-century recipe commences with three hundred and eighty-four oranges, and more recent ones have the addition of rum.

The wassail bowl requires port and sherry, sugar, nutmeg, mace, cinnamon, cloves and other spices. Egg yolks and whipped egg whites are whisked in; it is warmed until it froths; soft-roasted apples are floated on top and it is served hot. At Dingley Dell, Mr Pickwick and his friends sat down to supper 'and a mighty bowl of wassail . . . in which the hot apples were hissing and bubbling with a rich look and a jolly sound.'

Many people deplored the excessive over-eating and drinking that took place at Christmas as they felt that the quiet simplicity of the first Christmas was being lost and the festival had become merely an excuse for lavish over-indulgence. Lord Macaulay, the nineteenth-century writer, was not of this opinion as these verses show:

> *Though Quakers scowl, though Baptists howl,*
> *Though Plymouth Brethren rage,*
> *We Churchmen gay will wallow to-day*
> *In apple sauce, onions and sage.*
>
> *Ply knife and fork, and draw the cork,*
> *And have the bottle handy,*
> *For each slice of goose will introduce*
> *A thimbleful of brandy.*

But one contented man was Thomas Tusser who, in the mid-sixteenth century, wrote:

> *Good husband and huswife now cheefly be glad,*
> *Things handsome to have, as they ought to be had:*
> *They both doo provide against Christmas doo come,*
> *To welcome good neighbours, good cheare to have some,*
> *Good bread and good drinke, a good fier in the hall,*
> *Brawne, pudding and souse, and good mustard with all.*
> *Beefe, mutton, and porke, shred pies of the best,*
> *Pig, veale, goose, and capon, and turkey, well drest;*
> *Cheese, apples, and nuts, joly Carols to heare,*
> *As then in the countrie is counted good cheare,*
> *What cost to good husband is any of this?*
> *Good household provision onely it is*
> *Of other the like, I doo leave out a menie,*
> *That costeth the husbandman never a penie.*